The Bush Theatre

presents the UK premiere of

The Aliens

by Annie Baker

15 September – 15 October 2010

World premiere produced by Rattlestick Playwrights Theater
New York, April 2010

The Bush Theatre would like to give particular thanks to:
aka, West 12 Shopping Centre, Westfield London, Vesbar,
James Turner, Nick Spalding, Nick Jarvie.

Peter Gill directing at the Bush courtesy of the generous support
of John Shakeshaft

The Aliens

by Annie Baker

Cast

Evan	Olly Alexander
Jasper	Mackenzie Crook
KJ	Ralf Little

Creative Team

Director	Peter Gill
Designer	Lucy Osborne
Lighting Designer	David Holmes
Composer, Sound Designer	Terry Davies
Associate Sound Designer	Tom Gibbons
Assistant Director	Barney Norris
Stage Manager (on the book)	Robyn Hardy
Assistant Stage Manager	Adam McElderry
Wardrobe Supervisor	Liz Evans
Set Builder	Joe Schermoly
Scenic Artist	Bethany Ann McDonald

Company

Olly Alexander (Evan)

TV includes: *The Fades, Lewis: Allegory of Love, Summerhill.*

Film includes: *The Dish and the Spoon, Gulliver's Travels, Dust, Tormented, Bright Star, Enter The Void.*

Mackenzie Crook (Jasper)

Theatre includes: *Jerusalem* (Royal Court); *The Seagull* (Royal Court and Broadway); *The Exonerated* (Riverside Studios); *One Flew Over The Cuckoo's Nest* (Gielgud Theatre).

Television includes: *The Accused, Merlin, Skins, Demons, Little Dorrit, The Office, The 11 O'Clock Show.*

Film includes: *Ironclad, The Adventures of TinTin, Sex, Drugs and Rock 'n' Roll, Soloman Kane, 3 and Out, City of Ember, Pirates of the Caribbean 1, 2* and *3, Land of the Blind, The Merchant of Venice, Brothers Grimm, Churchill: The Hollywood Years, Sex Lives of the Potato Men, Finding Neverland, The Life and Death of Peter Sellers, Still Crazy, Ant Muzak.*

Ralf Little (KJ)

Theatre for the Bush includes: *50 Ways to Leave Your Lover.*

Other theatre includes: *Stacy* (Trafalgar Studios); *On The Ceiling* (Garrick); *Billy Liar* (ATG); *Notes on Falling Leaves, Presence* (Royal Court).

TV includes: *Married Single Other, Massive, Miss Marple, Robin Hood, Heartbeat, The Royle Family, Brief Encounters, Two Pints of Lager & A Packet of Crisps, The Eustace Bros, Pear Shaped North Face of the Eiger, Paradise Heights, The Bill, Always & Everyone, Flint Street Nativity, Bostockis Cup.*

Film includes: *Powder, Telstar, The Waiting Room, Frozen, 24 Hour Party People, Al's Lads.*

Annie Baker (Writer)

Annie Baker grew up in Amherst, Massachusetts. Her full-length plays include *Body Awareness* (Atlantic Theater Company, Drama Desk and Outer Critics Circle nominations for Best Play/Playwright); *Circle Mirror Transformation* (Playwrights Horizons, OBIE Award for Best New American Play, Drama Desk nomination for Best Play); *The Aliens* (Rattlestick Playwrights Theater, OBIE Award for Best New American Play); *The End of the Middle Ages* (commission for Soho Rep) and *Nocturama*. Her work has also been developed and produced at New York Theatre Workshop, MCC, Soho Rep, the Orchard Project, the Ontological-Hysteric, Ars Nova, the Huntington, South Coast Rep, the Magic Theater, the Cape Cod Theatre Project, the Bay Area Playwrights Festival and the Sundance Institute Theatre Lab in Utah and Ucross, Wyoming. Recent honors include a New York Drama Critics Circle Special Citation, a Susan Smith Blackburn Prize nomination, a Time Warner Storytelling Fellowship, a MacDowell Fellowship and commissions from Center Theatre Group and Playwrights Horizons.

Terry Davies (Composer, Sound Designer)

Terry started his professional composing at the National Theatre where he had been a music director and orchestrator. He first worked there as co-orchestrator of the multi-award winning *Guys and Dolls* and went on to work on some 32 productions. Alongside these have been scores for the Royal Shakespeare Company, Donmar Warehouse, Almeida, Royal Court and many other theatres.

In the recording studio Terry has conducted or orchestrated the music for many TV dramas as well as 47 feature films. Current among these are *The Illusionist* and Mike Leigh's *Another Year*. Original music for TV includes his score for *The Car Man* and the songs for *Tipping the Velvet* which gained him a BAFTA nomination. He is an associate artist of Matthew Bourne's New Adventures Company and he won an Olivier Award for his music for Matthew's *Play Without Words*.

Tom Gibbons (Associate Sound Designer)

Tom trained at Central School of Speech and Drama in Theatre Sound and is resident sound designer for the international physical theatre company Parrot{in the}Tank.

Recent design credits for Parrot include: Excursions (Arts Depot and Roundhouse); *Just Above The Below* (Arts Theatre, Paradise Gardens Festival, Tour of Slovakia); *Freeman Gallop* (ICA London, Prague Scenofest, Budva Montenegro); *Storm in a Teacup* (Arts Depot).

Other recent design credits include: *The Chairs* (Theatre Royal Bath); *The Country, The Road To Mecca, The Roman Bath, 1936, The Shawl* (Arcola); *50 Ways To Leave Your Lover, 50 Ways To Leave Your Lover@Xmas, Broken Space*

Season (Bush Theatre); *Everything Must Go, Soho Streets* (Soho Theatre); *Holes* (New Wimbledon Studio); *Terror Tales* (Hampstead Studio); *The Hostage, Present Tense* (Southwark Playhouse); Faustus (Watford Palace, Tour); *Faithless Bitches* (Courtyard); *FAT* (The Oval House); *Just Me Bell* (Graeae, Tour); *Blue Heaven* (Finborough);*Pitching In* (Latitude Festival, Tour); *Overspill, Shape Of Things, Old Man and The Sea, This Limetree Bower, Someone Who'll Watch Over Me* (Cockpit); *US Love Bites* (Old Red Lion, Tristan Bates); *I Can Sing A Rainbow with Nabokov and Sheffield Theatres* (Lyceum Sheffield); *Pendulum* (Jermyn Street); *Journalist and Hope* (ICA London); *Machinal* (Central); *Bar Of Ideas* (Paradise Gardens Festival and Glastonbury/Shangri-La).

Peter Gill (Director)

A hugely influential and radical figure in British theatre, Peter Gill is a renowned playwright and one of the most important directors of the last thirty years.

Peter Gill was born in 1939 in Cardiff and started his professional career as an actor. He has directed over a hundred productions in the UK, Europe and North America. At the Royal Court Theatre in the 1960s, he was responsible for introducing D. H. Lawrence's plays to the theatre and was the founding director of Riverside Studios and the Royal National Theatre Studio.

Classical plays directed include: *The Importance of Being Earnest* (Theatre Royal Bath, Tour & Vaudeville Theatre, 2008); *Gaslight* (Old Vic, 2007); *Look Back in Anger* (Theatre Royal Bath, 2006); *The Voysey Inheritance* (NT, 2006); *Romeo and Juliet* (RSC, 2004-05); *Uncle Vanya* (Field Day Tour, 1995); *The Way of the World* (Lyric Hammersmith, 1992); *The Cherry Orchard* (Riverside Studios, 1978); *The Changeling* (Riverside Studios, 1978) and *Twelfth Night* (RSC, 1974 / Aldwych, 1975)

New work directed includes: *Hens* (Sky Arts Live - Riverside Studios, 2010); *Semper Dowland, The Corridor* (Aldeburgh Festival / Southbank Centre, 2009); *Epitaph For George Dillon, Anthony Creighton* (ATG, 2005); *Days of Wine and Roses* (Donmar Warehouse, 2005); *Scenes from the Big Picture* (NT, 2003); *Speed the Plough* (ATG, 2000); *Tongue of a Bird* (Almeida, 1997); *New England* (RSC, 1994); *Mrs.Klein* (NT, 1988); *Tales from Hollywood* (NT, 1983).

Plays directed for the Royal Court include: *The Fool* (1975), *Crimes of Passion – The Ruffian on the Stair, The Erpingham Camp* (1966) and *A Collier's Friday Night* (1965).

As writer as well as director, Peter's plays include: *Another Door Closed* (Theatre Royal Bath, 2009); *Small Change* (Donmar Warehouse, 2008); *The York Realist* (English Touring Theatre at the Royal Court, 2002); *Original Sin* (Crucible Sheffield, 2002); *The Look Across the Eyes and Lovely Evening* (BBC Radio 4, 2001); *Certain Young Men* (Almeida, 1999); *Friendly Fire* (NT, 1998/99); *Cardiff East* (NT, 1995); *Mean Tears* (NT, 1987); *In the Blue* (NT, 1985); *Small Change* (NT, 1983); *Kick for Touch* (NT, 1983); *The Sleepers Den* (Royal Court, 1969) and *Over Gardens Out* (Royal Court, 1969).

David Holmes (Lighting Designer)

Theatre for the Bush includes: *Cruising.*

Other theatre includes: *Cat on a Hot Tin Roof* (Novello Theatre); *The Gods Weep* and *Days of Significance* (RSC); *Gurrelieder* (London Philharmonia Orchestra conducted by Esa-Pekka Salonen, Royal Festival Hall); *La Serva Padrona* and *To Hell and Back* (Opera Faber at the Viana do Castelo festival, Portugal); *Victory: Choices in Reaction* and *The Road to Mecca* (Arcola); *The Chairs* and *Gagarin Way* (Bath); *How to be an Other Woman* and *Things of Dry Hours* (The Gate); *Rusalka* (ETO); *Goalmouth* (The Sage, Gateshead); *Ma Vie En Rose* (Young Vic); *Alaska* (Royal Court); *Widowers' Houses, A Taste of Honey, See How They Run, Pretend You Have Big Buildings, Cyrano de Bergerac, Harvey* and *Roots* (Manchester Royal Exchange); *The Rise and Fall of Little Voice* and *Rope* (Watermill Theatre, Newbury); *Blood Wedding* (South Bank); *Sweetness and Badness* (WNO); *After Miss Julie, Othello, Woman In Mind* and *Be My Baby* (Salisbury); *TILT* (Traverse, Edinburgh); *Hortensia and the Museum of Dreams* (RADA); *Humble Boy* and *The 101 Dalmatians* (Northampton); *Stallerhof* (Southwark Playhouse); *Fijis* (Jean Abreu Dance at the South Bank Centre and The Place); *Inside* (Jean Abreu Dance); *The Leningrad Siege* (Wilton's Music Hall); *The Trestle at Pope Lick Creek* (Manchester Royal Exchange and Southwark Playhouse); *The Fantasticks, Ain't Misbehavin', House* and *Garden*, and *Cleo, Camping, Emmanuelle and Dick* (Harrogate); *The Secret Rapture* (Chichester); *Twelfth Night* (Cambridge); *Look Back In Anger* (Exeter); *Dov and Ali, The Water Engine, The Water Harvest, Photos of Religion* and *A State of Innocence* (Theatre 503).

David trained at the Theatre Royal, Glasgow and the Guildhall School of Music and Drama.

Barney Norris (Assistant Director)

Theatre as Director includes: *Small Change* (O'Reilly Theatre, Oxford); *Fanshen* (O'Reilly Theatre, Oxford); *Hamlet* (Wadham Chapel, Oxford).

Other theatre includes: *The School for Scandal* (Salisbury Playhouse); *Noye's Fludde* (Salisbury Cathedral/BBC4).

Barney's first play, *At First Sight*, won the Drama Association of Wales's One Act Play competition and will be produced in the New Year by theatre company Up In Arms. Barney has a degree in English from Oxford University, where he was Drama Officer (2009 – 10).

Lucy Osborne (Designer)

Theatre for the Bush includes: *Like a Fishbone, The Whisky Taster, If There Is I Haven't Found It Yet, Wrecks, Broken Space Season, Sea Wall, 2,000 Feet Away, Tinderbox* and *tHe dYsFUnCKshOnalZ!*

Recent theatre credits include *The Taming of the Shrew* and *Twelfth Night* (Chicago Shakespeare Theatre, for which she won Chicago 'Jeff Award' for Scenic Design); *Playhouse Live: Here* (Sky Arts); *Andersen's English, Dreams of Violence* (Out of Joint); *Shades* (Royal Court's Young Writers Festival); *Macbeth* (Edinburgh Lyceum/Nottingham Playhouse); *Nina* and *Gas Station Angel* (repertoire, LAMDA); *Timing* (Kings Head) and *When Romeo Met Juliet* (BBC).

She designed *Artefacts* (Nabakov Theatre Company / Bush) and *Some Kind of Bliss* (Trafalgar Studios), both of which transferred to the 2008 'Brits off Broadway Festival' in New York. Other theatre credits include *Be My Baby* (New Vic Theatre); *Rope* (Watermill Theatre); *Closer* (Theatre Royal Northampton); *The Long and the Short and The Tall* (Sheffield Lyceum); *The Prayer Room* (Birmingham Rep/Edinburgh Festival); *Ship of Fools* (Theatre 503); *The Unthinkable* (Sheffield Crucible Studio) and *Season of Migration to the North* (RSC New Writing Season).

Lucy is an Associate Artist at the Bush.

Michael Chernus, Patch Darragh and Erin Gann (Music and Lyrics)

Michael Chernus, Patch Darragh and Erin Gann are actor/musicians who live in New York City. They started writing songs together in 1998 while attending the Juilliard School. Between 1998 and 2002 they wrote over 150 trippy folk songs under the moniker 'The Greens'. Once in a while, they'd play NYC venues like Galapagos or The Raccoon Lodge.

The Bush Theatre

'One of the most experienced prospectors of raw talent in Europe'
The Independent

Since its inception in 1972, the Bush Theatre has pursued its singular vision of discovery, risk and entertainment from its home on the corner of Shepherds Bush Green. That vision is valued and embraced by a community of audience and artists radiating out from our distinctive corner of West London across the world. The Bush is a local theatre with an international reputation. From its beginning, the Bush has produced hundreds of groundbreaking premieres, many of them Bush commissions, and hosted guest productions by leading companies and artists from across the world. On any given night, those queuing at the foot of our stairs to take their seats could have travelled from Auckland or popped in from round the corner.

What draws them to the Bush is the promise of a good night out and our proven commitment to launch, from our stage, successive generations of playwrights and artists. Samuel Adamson, David Eldridge, Jonathan Harvey, Catherine Johnson, Tony Kushner, Stephen Poliakoff, Jack Thorne and Victoria Wood (all then unknown) began their careers at the Bush. The unwritten contract between talent and risk is understood by actors who work at the Bush, creating roles in untested new plays. Unique amongst local theatres, the Bush consistently draws actors of the highest reputation and calibre. Joseph Fiennes and Ian Hart recently took leading roles in a first play by an unknown playwright to great critical success. John Simm and Richard Wilson acted in premieres both of which transferred into the West End. The Bush has won over 100 awards, and developed an enviable reputation for touring its acclaimed productions nationally and internationally. Audiences and organisations far beyond our stage profit from the risks we take. The value attached to the Bush by other theatres and by the film and television industries is both significant and considerable. The Bush receives more than 1,000 scripts through the post every year, and reads and responds to them all. This is one small part of a comprehensive playwrights' development programme which nurtures the relationship between writer and director, as well as playwright residencies and commissions.

Everything that we do to develop playwrights focuses them towards a production on our stage or beyond. We have also launched an ambitious new education, training and professional development programme, bushfutures, providing opportunities for different sectors of the community and professionals to access the expertise of Bush playwrights, directors, designers, technicians and actors, and to play an active role in influencing the future development of the theatre and its programme. Last year saw the launch of our new social networking and online publishing website www.bushgreen.org. The site is a great new forum for playwrights and theatre people to meet, share experiences and collaborate.

Through this pioneering work, the Bush will reach and connect with new writers and new audiences, and find new plays to stage.

Josie Rourke, Artistic Director

At the Bush Theatre

We're a full-time staff of eleven, supported by a big team of associates, interns, and freelancers. For ways to get involved, please look at our website www.bushtheatre.co.uk

***Artistic Director**	Josie Rourke
Executive Director	Angela Bond
Development Director	Trish Wadley

Box Office and Front of House Manager	Annette Butler
Marketing Manager	Sophie Coke-Steel
Producer	Caroline Dyott
Assistant to the Directors	Liz Eddy
Technical Manager	Neil Hobbs
Development Manager	Bethany Ann McDonald
Production Manager	Anthony Newton
Associate Director – bushfutures	Anthea Williams

Assistant Technician	Samuel Charleston
Bookkeeper	Ella Rule
Development Officer	Leonora Twynam

Associateships, Internships and Attachments

Associate Directors	Nathan Curry
	Charlotte Gwinner
Pearson Writer in Residence	Nick Payne
Composer on attachment	Michael Bruce
Apprentice	Sade Banks
bushfutures Intern	Lucy McCann
Associate Playwright	Anthony Weigh
Creative Associates	Joe Murphy, Nessah Muthy,
	Richard Twynam, Ed Viney.
Associate Artists	Tanya Burns, Arthur Darvill,
	Chloe Emmerson, James Farncombe,
	Richard Jordan, Emma Laxton,
	Paul Miller, Lucy Osborne
Box Office Assistants	Kirsty Cox, Alex Hern, Kate McGregor,
	Ava Jade Morgan, Sade Banks,
	Karim Morgan, Dervla Toal
	Sade Banks, Kirsty Cox, Alex Hern,
Front of House Duty Managers	Lucy McCann, Kirsty Patrick Ward,
	Chrissy Angus, Annie Jenkins,
	Amanda Ramasawmy,
Duty Technicians	Ben Ainsley, Ruth Perrin
Press Representative	Ewan Thomson
Press Assistant	Ava Jade Morgan
Bush Interns	Christina Angus, Mary Franklin
Production Intern	Aaron Porter

* **Bold** text indicates full time staff, regular indicates part time/temporary.

The Bush Theatre, Shepherds Bush Green, London W12 8QD
Box Office: 020 8743 5050 | www.bushtheatre.co.uk

The Alternative Theatre Company Ltd. (The Bush Theatre)
is a Registered Charity no. 270080

Company registration no. 1221968 | VAT no. 228 3168 73

Supported by
**ARTS COUNCIL
ENGLAND**

supported by
h&f
hammersmith & fulham

Be There at the Beginning

The Bush Theatre would like to say a very special 'Thank You' to the following supporters, corporate sponsors and trusts and foundations, whose valuable contributions continue to help us nurture, develop and present some of the brightest new literary stars and theatre artists.

If you are interested in finding out how to be involved, visit the 'Support Us' section of our website, email development@bushtheatre.co.uk or call 020 8743 3584.

The Bush Theatre has recently launched **bushgreen**, a social networking website for people in theatre to connect, collaborate and publish plays in innovative ways. The mission of **bushgreen** is to connect playwrights with theatre practitioners and plays with producers, to promote best practice and to inspire the creation of exciting new theatre.

bushgreen allows members to:

- Submit plays directly to the Bush for our team to read and consider for production

- Connect with other writers, directors, producers and theatres

- Publish scripts online so more people can access your work

- Purchse scripts from hundreds of new playwrights

There are thousands of members and hundreds of plays on the site.

To join, log on to **www.bushgreen.org**

Bush Theatre Greening

The Bush Theatre is committed to greening itself to improve its environmental sustainability and reduce its carbon emissions.

We are doing this through a variety of practices including:

- reducing materials used by reusing and recycling all parts of our sets

- keeping all props and costume for reuse and loan to other productions

- looking carefully at the green credentials of all our suppliers

Our recent production of Anthony Weigh's play *Like a Fishbone* used a lighting rig which consumed approximately 64% less electricity than the previous production.

Our last production, *The Great British Country Fete*, had a set of which around 90% of materials were recycled from other events and productions.

The Bush is one of the first venues to be working with the Theatre's Trust ECOVENUE programme. The project provides specialist environmental advice and works with venues to create and develop environmental policies, offering assistance in monitoring energy, water use and waste diversion and procurement.

We are also working with the brilliant Julie's Bicycle (www.juliesbicycle.com) to develop schemes that green our work and to share these initiatives with other London theatres.

Why not help us expand this work by making a donation to The Bush?

For more information visit **www.bushtheatre.co.uk/support/**

Annie Baker
The Aliens

original music and lyrics by
Michael Chernus, Patch Darragh
and Erin Gann

faber and faber

First published in 2010
by Faber and Faber Ltd
The Bindery, 51 Hatton Garden
London EC1N 8HN

Typeset by Country Setting, Kingsdown, Kent CT14 8ES
Printed and bound by CPI Group (UK) Ltd, Croydon, CR0 4YY

A CIP record for this book
is available from the British Library

978-0-571-27444-4

Printed and bound in the UK on FSC® certified paper in line with our continuing
commitment to ethical business practices, sustainability and the environment.
For further information see faber.co.uk/environmental-policy

Our authorised representative in the EU for product safety is
Easy Access System Europe, Mustamäe tee 50, 10621 Tallinn, Estonia
gpsr.requests@easproject.com

Characters

Jasper
thirty-one

KJ
thirty

Evan
seventeen

At least a third of this play is silence.
Pauses should be at least three seconds long.
Silences should last from five to ten seconds.
Long pauses and long silences should,
of course, be even longer.

'Andrea' is pronounced 'Ahn-DREY-a'

A slash (/) indicates the point of overlap
where the next speech begins.

THE ALIENS

Act One

The desolate back patio of a coffee shop in Vermont.
A recycling bin. A trash bin. A 'PLEASE USE THE FRONT
ENTRANCE' *sign.*
    Jasper and KJ are sitting in the sun at a lone picnic
table, their feet up on plastic chairs. KJ has a beard and
long hair pulled into a messy bun. Jasper has shorter hair
and simmers with quiet rage. He wears sweatpants and
sandals.
    Jasper is smoking. KJ is drinking a to-go cup of tea.
A long silence.
    Eventually KJ starts singing to himself.

KJ (*sings*)
    I won't
    Waste away
    Wondering why
    I won't go down like that
    If I die
    Time machines were made for me
    I believe
    Impossibilities
    Are what you perceive
    Triple-dimensional superstar
    Triple-dimensional superstar
    Triple-dimensional superstar.

Jasper smokes. A pause.

I'm a Martian masterpiece
From another dimension
Time and space weren't meant for me.
No I'm not down with that.

Triple-dimensional superstar
Triple-dimensional superstar
Triple-dimensional superstar.

Jasper smokes. A long silence. KJ drinks his tea. Then:

Remember Orion?

Jasper nods.

He started a wind farm.
Near Marshfield.

Jasper exhales.

Jasper What does that mean, he started a wind farm?

KJ He started a wind farm. He lives on a wind farm.

Jasper Wind farm like the big / white –

KJ The big white spinny things.

Pause.

With like the – on top of a mountain or something.

Jasper Aren't those owned by the government?

KJ I don't know. He lives on one.

Jasper Yeah, but it's not . . . it's just like a bunch of wheels by the side of the road.

KJ Yeah.

Pause.

Jasper So how does he live on one?

KJ He just does.

Jasper Who told you that?

KJ . . . Eli.

Jasper sighs and stubs out his cigarette. KJ watches him, worried.

Another long silence.

Hey. Uh. Do you wanna talk about it? Or would you rather just, uh . . .

KJ trails off.

Jasper Andrea?

KJ nods.

Not really.

KJ nods again. A pause.

She's crazy, man.

KJ nods again. A pause.

It's sad. I mean, it's really fucking sad.

A pause.

There's actually something wrong with her.

KJ Like –

Jasper Like borderline paranoia or something. Some kind of psychological issue.

KJ nods.

So it's actually kind of a relief. It feels like a relief.

KJ Cool.

Jasper And ah . . . I don't know. She played games, you know? She was into that shit. She was into Power. And like . . . part of me found it attractive but it was also really / uh –

KJ That's not good, man.

Jasper And uh . . . you know, her thing was like . . . that she didn't have a personality any more? That she'd like 'lost her personality'. In the shadow of my . . .

But the hilarious thing is that she was the one who like fucking glued herself to my hip. I didn't need that, man. Necessarily. But she made us that. While like still attempting to fuck with my head the whole time and make me feel like shit.

A pause. KJ nods again, at a loss. Jasper lights another cigarette.

KJ I'm sorry.

Jasper Don't say you're sorry. It's a good thing.

Pause.

I don't need to talk about it.

Pause.

I actually feel bad for her.

KJ watches Jasper, who smokes and refuses to look at KJ. After a while KJ starts squinting up at the sun and opening his mouth a little.

Jasper What're you doing?

KJ (*still squinting*) . . . Trying to sneeze.

Jasper What is that / supposed to –

KJ It helps you sneeze.
Looking at the sun helps you sneeze.

Jasper watches KJ try to sneeze for a while. KJ is unsuccessful. Eventually he goes back to sipping his tea.
A long silence.
Jasper suddenly kicks a plastic chair over. It makes a terrible noise.

Whoa.

Five seconds later, the back door to the coffee shop opens. Evan peeks his head out the door, sees them,

then steps outside, in his white apron. Evan is
seventeen and in a constant state of humiliation.

Evan Hey.
Um . . .

Jasper and KJ regard him coldly.

Hey.
We're not allowed to, uh . . .

Pause.

Did you guys just kick that chair over?

Jasper and KJ do not respond. Evan waits, in agony,
then:

Um. So. We're not allowed to . . . people aren't actually
supposed to sit out here.
It's uh, it's like a staff area. You're supposed to sit at
the tables out front.

Jasper Who are you?

Evan Um. I'm Evan.

Jasper You new here?

Evan Uh . . . yeah.

KJ We know Rahna.

Evan . . . Okay . . .

Pause.

KJ Rahna lets us sit out here.

Evan Um. Okay. Uh.
Because I was told that we should not, um . . . that
under no / condition –

Jasper What's your last name?

Evan Shelmerdine.

KJ *Shel*merdine?

Jasper . . . 'Cause you look like this girl I know. You look like you could be her younger brother.

Evan doesn't know what to say.

Emily.

Evan Okay. Cool. Yeah, I don't have a sister named Emily.

Jasper Her last name is Spencer.

Pause.

Evan Um . . . would it be okay with you guys to move out front? 'Cause it's my second day working here, and I really don't want to get in, um, trouble.

They both look at him and do not move. Evan stands there for a while. Like ten seconds. Everyone is very still.
 Finally Evan turns around and walks back inside. After a while:

KJ Does it feel hot to you?
 Like especially hot?

Jasper doesn't respond.

Is it supposed to be this hot in June?

Jasper It's July.

KJ Oh yeah?

Jasper July 2nd.

Pause.

KJ He was like *twelve*. That kid.

Pause.

July 2nd. That makes sense.

'Cause the other night I heard like . . . preparations or whatever. People were like setting off fireworks in their backyard.

Pause.

Have you noticed that? That everybody always starts practising like the week before the Fourth of July? Why do they need to practise?

Pause.

Don't they just *light* it?

Jasper doesn't answer. He touches the pack of cigarettes in his pocket. He drums his fingers on the table.
After a while, he gets up, rights the plastic chair he kicked over and sits back down.
KJ basks in the sun.
Blackout.

SCENE TWO

The next day. KJ is sitting by himself at the table. He has another to-go cup of tea. He removes his tea bag from his cup, opens it, pours out a little bit of the tea onto the plastic table, removes a tiny packet from his pocket and refills the tea bag with the contents of the tiny packet. Somewhere during this careful operation Evan comes out the back door in his apron, beleaguered, dragging a huge garbage bag behind him.

He sees KJ, tries to figure out whether or not to say anything, then lifts up the lid of the garbage bin and dumps the garbage bag in.

KJ turns around, sees him, waves cheerfully and then goes back to his tea-bag surgery.

Evan, for lack of a better response, waves back. Then he wipes his hands on his apron and watches KJ. After a while:

Evan Don't you mind the smell back here?

KJ *(not looking up)* Can't smell a thing, my brother.

Pause.

Evan . . . So Rahna doesn't actually work here any more.

No response. KJ twists the new tea bag together and puts it back in his cup. Then he takes a small wooden stirrer out of his pocket and starts stirring.
Evan looks at the mess on the table.

What are you doing?

KJ Concocting.

KJ blows on the tea, then tastes it. He smiles.

Taste it.

Evan looks dubious, then walks forward, takes the cup, and takes a tiny sip. He nods and hands it back. A pause.

You go to SHS?

Evan Yes. I mean. I have one more year left.

KJ Is Mr Amato still around?

Evan *(nervously glancing back towards the door)* Yeah. Um. I had him for World Civ this past year. He's cool.

KJ I *hate* that guy.

Evan doesn't know how to respond.

He's still there?!

Evan nods.

Oh fuck. Someone needs to fucking *kill* that guy.
That guy ruined my life.
Shit. Just thinking about him makes me wanna like –
Oh man!
That guy is such a *bitch*!

KJ sips his tea and tries to calm down. Evan hovers for a moment, not sure what to do, and then goes back inside. The door shuts behind him.
KJ sits by himself for a while. He drinks his tea. Then KJ takes out his cell phone and dials.

(*After a pause.*) Where are you?

Pause.

Ah yes.

Pause.

You are on fire, my friend.

He listens while we hear Jasper's voice, quiet at first, get louder and louder as he approaches the patio from a distance and then arrives, scaling/pushing his way through any fences/shrubs in his way.

Jasper . . . And then I realised that he goes to California. And he drives up the coast. And he's got like five bucks to his name but back then that was like fifty bucks. And he drives, right, he drives up the coast and he sees the ocean for the first time in his life. And then he drives to Big Sur. Which is where . . . that's where Henry Miller lived.

Jasper has now reached KJ. They see each other and snap their cell phones shut.

So Miller's gonna be a character.

KJ No shit.

Jasper Very minor. But he makes an appearance.

Jasper hauls off his backpack and sits down. He looks at the mess on the table.

Shroom tea?

KJ Myfriendmyfriend.

Jasper sits down and takes out his cigarettes. He lights one. He seems wound up.
    They sit there.
    Eventually KJ starts singing.

Two fixed points is a constant
Two focal points are the same point
Eccentricity is identical
The X-axis is perpendicular
The graph drawn
Is lateral
The equation
Is literal
Write the equation
In intercept form
Ratio is symmetry
Is constant
Is symmetry
The turning point is also
The axis
Of symmetry
Equidistant from the focus
An ellipse
Is the locus
The eccentricity of the ellipse
Is blossomed lotus.

Jasper smokes agitatedly and stares off into the distance. After a while KJ gets out of his chair, lies

*down on the ground on his back, and elevates his legs
on his plastic chair.*

. . . Back problems.

Jasper Oh yeah?

KJ I slept on it weird.

A long pause. Jasper smokes. Suddenly:

Jasper Did you know that Andrea started dating that
guy? You did, didn't you? You don't have to hide it from
me or anything. I'm actually happy about it.

Pause.

KJ Wait, what?!

Jasper She's dating that guy. Sprocket.
She's dating a guy named Sprocket.

KJ I had no idea.

Jasper It's cool if you did, man.

KJ I had No Fucking Idea. I swear to God.

Pause.

Who's Sprocket?!

Jasper The tall guy? With the hair? At Noah's party?

Pause.

He makes his own pants?

KJ Oh God.

Jasper He takes like that fucking Chinese kimono cloth
and sews his own pants or something and everybody
makes a big fucking deal about it?

KJ Oh man.

17

Pause.

Sprocket.

Jasper stubs out his cigarette.

Jasper His real name is probably like *Barnaby* or something.

KJ Ha.
Yes.

Jasper So you didn't know.

KJ . . . I did not know.

Jasper She called me to tell me. Last night.
'In case I saw them together.'

Short pause.

I'm telling you, it ended up being one of the best nights of my life. I was just doing nothing, fucking staring out window, and then I get this phone call, and she has this like haughty tone, and she's like telling me that . . .
Hold on.

Jasper suddenly leans forward, rests his elbow on his knees, and bows his head. KJ, who is still lying on his back, lifts his head up a little and peers over.

KJ Are you okay?

Jasper Yeah. I just had to, like, breathe.

KJ Whoa.

Jasper I feel fantastic, though.

KJ, his head still raised, continues to peer over at Jasper, but after a little while his neck gets tired and he puts his head back down.
Jasper takes a deep breath and collects himself.

Wow. That was like a crazy head-rush-slash-heart-attack.
Okay.
So she calls me and delivers The Big News or whatever in the most condescending freakish manner possible, and I call her a cunt, which, if you recall, was like the big no-no word in our relationship, and she says, 'You promised never to call me that again,' and I say 'ARE YOU ACTUALLY LISTENING TO YOURSELF?' and I hang up.
And then for like five minutes I'm like . . .
Worst five minutes of my life.
Actually. No. Not the worst five minutes of my life.
Bad, though.

KJ What were the worst five minutes of your life?

Jasper (*ignoring him*) BUT THEN.
I remember something Your. Fucking. Mother. Told me. Over dinner.

KJ Sandy Jano?!

Jasper I remember something Sandy Jano told me. She said it like three years ago. When I crashed on your couch.

KJ Oh yeah.

Jasper I was like talking to her about how I was always like getting kicked out of places and like sleeping on floors or whatever and she was like: this, uh, this in-between state, this being unstable or whatever, if you accept / it –

KJ Oh man. Was she talking about her gender stuff?

Jasper No. No. She was like: the state of just having lost something is like the most enlightened state in the world.

KJ is silent.

And I thought of that last night, and all of a sudden I felt like incredible. I was simultaneously like being stabbed in the heart over and over again with this like devil knife but I also felt *euphoric*.

And then I sat down and I wrote like twenty pages.

KJ In one night?

Jasper And they were like . . . the book just . . . it just switched in a totally different direction. He leaves Iowa City! The whole thing was supposed to take place in Iowa City and he leaves! He's goin' to California!

Pause.

KJ Awesome.

KJ lifts his legs off the chair and tries to bring his knees down to his chest with some difficulty.

Jasper, trying to hide his disappointment at KJ's lack of a response, takes out another cigarette and lights it.

Evan comes out the back door with a final bag of trash, no apron on, crippled under the weight of a huge L. L. Bean backpack.

Jasper Shelmerdine!

Evan nods, trying to look dignified, and throws the bag into the dumpster.

How are you today, Shelmerdine?

Evan Um. I'm good.
Takin' off.

Jasper You done already?

Evan Um. Yeah. Eight to three.

Jasper . . . You smoke?

Evan Um.
Occasionally.
I don't know.

Jasper Want one?

Evan (*after glancing behind him at the door*) Uh . . .
sure.

> *Jasper offers him a cigarette. Evan takes it and holds*
> *it between two slightly trembling fingers. Jasper holds*
> *out a lighter. After a half-second of confusion, Evan*
> *remembers what to do, leans forward, inhales, lights*
> *it, and then steps back.*
> *He smokes passably, taking tiny hits, still wearing*
> *his backpack.*
> *Jasper smokes.*
> *KJ is still lying on his back.*
> *After a while:*

KJ Will someone please pass the psilocybin tea?

> *Jasper ignores him.*

Will someone please pass the psilocybin tea?

> *Jasper takes KJ's cup of tea and carefully pours it out*
> *onto the ground.*

Evan What's psilocybum?

Jasper He's obsessed with incorporating shrooms into
every food group.

KJ Shroom karaoke.

> *KJ laughs. No one else does.*

Evan Wait. That tea has mushrooms in it? Psychedelic
mushrooms?

> *Jasper nods.*

He gave me some. He made me drink some!

Jasper How much?

Evan Like a whole sip.

Jasper You're fine.

Evan Shit!

Jasper You're fine.

Evan Do I seem weird?

Jasper Do you feel weird?

A pause while Evan tries to gauge if he feels weird.

Evan No. I don't know.

Jasper You're fine.

Pause.

Evan My friend grew up in Medfield? Massachusetts? And he said there was this guy at his school who like ate a bunch of shrooms and then tied his own hands to a radiator.

Pause.

And then they melted off.

KJ (*still on his back*) Urban myth.

Evan throws his cigarette on the ground and stubs it out with his sneaker, with some difficulty.

Evan Uh. I should probably head home.

Pause.

Um. What are your names? If you don't mind me asking.

Jasper I'm Jasper.

They both look over at KJ. His eyes are closed.

And that's KJ.

Evan Cool.
Um.

Cool. Yeah.

Um. If you guys like . . . if like my manager like comes in later and sees you guys and gets mad, don't tell him I saw you. I mean, I didn't know about it.

Jasper All right.

Evan Cool.

Jasper You just working here at The Green Sheep all summer, Shelmerdine?

Evan Uh. Yeah. Pretty much. I'm gone next week. But then I'm back.

Jasper Where you goin'?

Evan Uh . . .
I'm a . . . I'm working as a C-I-T?

Jasper A what?

Evan Counsellor-in-Training? It's just like a week-long thing.

Jasper At a camp?

Evan Uh . . . yeah.

Jasper What kind of camp?

This is the question Evan has been dreading.

Evan Uh . . . it's a, uh . . .
It's a Jewish music camp?
Um –

Jasper Jewish *music* camp?

Evan . . . Yeah.
Um.
I like teach little kids how to play piano and guitar and stuff.

Jasper Little Jewish kids.

Evan . . . Yeah. Um. My mom is Jewish.

Jasper thinks about this, then nods.

I went there when I was a little kid.

KJ You play guitar?

Evan No. Not . . . kinda. Not that well. Um. More piano.

KJ Jasper plays guitar.

Jasper rolls his eyes.

Evan Oh yeah?

Jasper I taught myself from, like, a book once.

KJ We had a band!

Jasper KJ thinks we had a band.
I'm actually a novelist now. I'm writing a novel.

Evan Oh. Cool.

KJ We had a band!

Evan What was the name of the band?

Jasper Oh fuck. Don't get him started.

KJ finally sits up.

KJ We had many names. Many phases. Many incarnations.

Jasper We could never agree on a name. We had like fifty different band names.

KJ The New Humans!

Jasper Yeah. He really pushed for that one.

KJ Hieronymous Blast.

Jasper Oh God.

KJ Pillowface.
Frog Men.
Electric Hookah.
The Limp Handshakes.
Joseph Yoseph.

Jasper 'Cause his great-grandfather was named Josef and mine was named Joseph.

KJ The JK/KJ Experience.

Jasper Because he's Kevin Jano and I'm Jasper Kopatch.

KJ The JK/KJ *Experiment*.

Jasper shakes his head.

Killer Jamball and the Jolly Kangaroo!
Dharma Machine!
Nefarious Hookah!

Jasper I wanted us to be called The Aliens.

KJ No. Boring.

Jasper After the Bukowski poem. You like Bukowski?

Evan Um . . . I don't know him. I don't know his stuff.

Jasper You ever write poetry?

Evan Um. No. I don't know. Not really. In my journal?
Sometimes?
No.

Jasper You gotta read Bukowski.

Evan Okay.

Jasper He cuts away all the bullshit.

Evan Cool.

Evan nods, and keeps nodding.

. . . Bukowski.

Jasper What are you doin' tomorrow night, Shelmerdine?

Evan Ah –

Jasper You goin' to the fireworks?

Evan Uh. I don't know. Maybe. I might just stay home.

Short pause.

Sometimes the Fourth, like, depresses me.

Jasper Oh yeah?

Evan Yeah. You know. I don't know. It's like all these families spread out on the football field? With the glowsticks? And they have that crappy local marching band. I don't know. It's like anticlimactic I guess? Like afterwards everyone seems a little disappointed. And I don't know: it's like, kind of random. Like we explode stuff in the sky and we look at it in like a group?

Pause.

And like, I kind of hate America. So I don't feel this like urgent need to celebrate it or anything.

A pause. Jasper nods thoughtfully.

Not that there's like . . . not like it's a bad thing . . . or like . . .

Evan trails off.

Jasper KJ and I are thinking of having a small shindig tomorrow night.

KJ A hootenanny.

Jasper We might read shit out loud. Sing a few songs. Although drumming circles are strictly forbidden.

KJ Drumming of any kind.

Evan Oh. Cool.

Jasper You could join us.

A pause.

Evan Um . . .
Yeah! Okay. Thanks.
Yeah.
Awesome.

Jasper We'll see you then, nine o'clock-ish.

Evan Um . . . where? Sorry. Where is the party?

Jasper Here.

Evan Oh. Um.
We're really not supposed to . . .
You can't have a party back here.

Jasper stares at him.

It's like a loitering thing.

Jasper I thought you guys were closed tomorrow.

Evan Yeah. We are. But it's. We're not supposed to. Be
here. Loiter here.

Jasper Fine.
Don't come.
It's not a big deal.

A pause while Evan stands there, at a loss.

No need to fret, little man.

Evan I just don't know if I can do it.

Jasper It's cool.

Evan Yeah. Um . . .

Jasper has gone cold. Evan sighs, re-shoulders his backpack and starts to walk away.

KJ (*sincerely*) Have fun at band camp!

Evan Uh.
. . . Thanks.

Evan hesitates again, then exits. Silence for a while. KJ is still lying on his back. He starts humming. Finally:

Jasper KJ.

KJ Yes.

Pause.

Jasper Are you freaking out?

KJ What?!
No!

Jasper You have to tell me if you start feeling weird again, man.

KJ No way.

A pause.

You know what Sandy Jano would say you're doing?

Jasper What?

KJ *Projecting*, man. You're projecting.

Jasper nods bleakly and stares off into the distance. After a while he reaches for his cigarettes. Blackout.

SCENE THREE

The next evening. The Fourth of July. Twilight. The sky turns dark as the scene progresses. There is a guitar case lying inconspicuously in the corner. Jasper is perched on

top of the recycling bin, reading aloud from a wrinkled
sheaf of paper. KJ is sitting in one of the plastic chairs,
wearing sunglasses, listening. He is rapt. Jasper is in the
middle of a sentence.

Jasper . . . and her bedroom smelled faintly of stale piss
and those porcelain bowls of dried rose petals his mother
used to put on the back of the toilet, before she died on
his fifteenth birthday.

Candace walked over to the window, took a long white
plastic rod between her fingers, and twisted it. Sunlight
flooded the dusty little room.

'What?' she said, grinning at him. 'I got nothing to be
ashamed of.' He noticed for the first time that her front
tooth was chipped, just a little. The right one. Something
about that tooth stirred him, made his gut ache.

She had the reddest hair he'd ever seen. It was a
dangerous red. It told you to stop and it told you to go
at the same time.

She turned around and faced him while he squinted
in the sunlight. She stared at him for a while, her eyes
moving up and down his face. Then she slowly started
rolling her T-shirt up. Her stomach was round and soft,
so pale it was almost translucent, with a cluster of tiny
hairs below the bellybutton. He surprised himself in that
moment by wishing for Allison, for her skinny, childish
body, her watery brown eyes, and the way she would
sleep with her head pressed so hard against his chest that
he'd wake up with bruises in the morning.

But here was Candace, right in front of him, ample
and ready, with her flaming torch hair and her ironic
smile. She pulled the T-shirt up all the way over her head
and revealed two large, pendulous white breasts. Her
nipples were big and pink and undefined, like they'd been
painted on with watercolours.

'Do you like me?' she asked. 'Do you like the way I
look?'

'I do,' he said, 'I do,' and he moved towards her / and –

KJ Holy shit, man. Your novel is turning me on.

Jasper puts down the paper and sighs.

I mean, it's amazing. It's great literature. It's just giving me a tiny bit of a boner.
Please. Continue.

Jasper gives him a stern look, then goes back to the piece of paper.

Jasper 'I do,' he said, 'I do,' and he moved towards her and grasped her hair with his hand, pulling her head back so her mouth opened a little. She let / out a –

KJ Oh wait. One thing.
Sorry.
Can I say one thing?

Jasper Yes.

KJ The thing about the fifteenth birthday?
I feel like . . . I feel like maybe it's like too much of a coincidence? That his mom died on his fifteenth birthday. It feels like . . . I'm supposed to be like, whoa, or something.

Jasper My mom died on my fifteenth birthday.

Pause.

KJ She did?

Jasper Yes. You knew that.

KJ Whoa. No.
I knew that you were . . . I knew that you were fifteen, man.
I didn't know it was on your birthday.

Jasper It was on my birthday.

KJ Jesus.
Oh man. That's horrible.
Wow.
Never mind.

A weird pause.

I'm sorry I didn't know you back then.

Jasper You should be thankful you didn't know me back then.

KJ (*shaking his head*) Jesus. On your birthday.

Jasper I would've kicked your ass.

KJ looks slightly wounded. He takes off his sunglasses and puts them in his lap.

Okay. I'm gonna skip ahead.

KJ No!

Jasper Yes.

Jasper flips through the pages.

This next part is what I wrote the other night.
After Andrea called.

Short pause.

By the way, she's left me like five messages since then and I haven't returned any of them.

Another short pause.

Okay.

Jasper starts reading again.

He was seeing America for the first time. In a way he'd been thinking about this drive since he was a kid, this drive across America. What did Arizona look like, he used to wonder. Utah? Wyoming? Oklahoma? Illinois?

He had imagined, somehow, that each state had a different set of plants and animals, a slightly different colour blue in the sky. But as he drove, as his little Hudson Hornet cranked and moaned across the long flat highways, and he flashed by farm after farm, cornfield after cornfield, desolate truck stop after desolate truck stop with the red flashing lights and the toothless man behind the counter and the occasional lonely woman with crinkled eyes desperately trying to catch his attention, as he crossed state line after state line, he realised that most of America looked like . . . most of America.

At this point Evan quietly and nervously enters, over the fence or through the shrubs, wearing his backpack. Jasper doesn't pause or seem to notice him. Evan stands near the edge of the patio, listening.

It was beautiful, sure, it moved him, but it repeated itself.

You could find the same thing there that you could find here.

And so as he approached California, his dream of California started to fade. He thought of what Miller had told him about the jutting cliffs in Big Sur, the mystical fog, the amethyst waves. But what if it was a lie? Or worse, some kind of delusion? What if Miller was actually living in a cornfield, sleeping on a billboard, writing underneath the glow of another drive-through movie theatre?

He not only started to doubt America, but he started to doubt himself. He started doubting the gift that Allison claimed he was born with.

She had first whispered that word a year and half ago, that strange, sacred word, she had whispered it into his ear one morning, and it had sent thrill and terror down his spine.

Genius.

She had breathed the word out, like a sigh, tickling his hair.

And immediately he knew she was right, he'd known it since he was a boy, that word had lived in him before he even knew how to say it or spell it, but after Allison had confronted him with it, made it live in the air, he started to feel a constant, pressing weight on his shoulders and his back.

The loneliness of it.

The loneliness of it could kill him.

He wasn't sure if he believed in a God, but if there was one, He was waiting up there in the sky impatiently, He was putting his finger on his watch and raising his eyebrows and saying:

'When's the new painting gonna be finished, son?'

'When you gonna stop fucking around?'

Jasper puts the sheaf of papers down. Everyone is very still.

Anyway.

I don't want to like bore you guys or anything.

Hello, Shelmerdine.

KJ leaps to his feet with an uncharacteristic amount of energy.

KJ WHAT THE FUCK?!

Jasper tries not to beam.

Whatthefuckwhatthefuckwhatthefuck. Oh my God.

KJ does a little prayer jog around the recycling bin.

Ohmygodohmygodohmygodohmygod.

Ohmygodohmygodohmygodohmygod.

Evan . . . That was really cool.

Jasper Aw, come on, Shelmerdine.

Evan That was really really cool.

Pause.

What's, um, what's the main character's name?

Jasper He doesn't have one.

Evan Oh. Cool.

Pause.

And uh . . . what's the title?

Jasper *Little Tigers Everywhere.*

Evan *Little Tigers Everywhere.* Cool.

Jasper It's from a Bukowski poem. It's the one that starts out 'Sam the whorehouse man / has squeaky shoes'?

Pause.

Evan Yeah. I don't know, um. I don't know. I mean, I'm gonna get him out from the library.

Pause. Evan hauls his backpack off and puts it down on the ground. It is somehow an important gesture. Maybe because it is the first time he is asserting himself as here.

KJ Yes!
Welcome to the Fourth of July!

Jasper Lookit that. Shelmerdine showed up. (*To KJ.*) Are you surprised?

KJ Fuck no. Fuck no.

Evan Is anyone else coming?

KJ and Jasper suddenly look self-conscious.

Jasper Uh . . . no.
Eli is being an asshole tonight and going out with – no.

KJ What's Noah doing?

Jasper . . . Being an asshole.

Pause.

Evan Um. I brought some stuff.

Evan kneels down and unzips his backpack.

Uh.

He removes some Tupperware.

Brownies. Um. My mom made like three batches of
brownies yesterday for some reason.
   Uh.
   . . . And this was the only thing I could steal. We don't
really have a, um, liquor cabinet. Um.

He takes a bottle out of his backpack.

Peppermint Schnapps?

KJ Ooh. *Peppermint.*

Jasper snatches the bottle out of Evan's hand.

Jasper I'll take that.

Jasper shoves the bottle into his pocket.

KJ Aw come on. Are you serious?

Jasper Yes.

KJ It's the Fourth of fucking July! I can drink Peppermint
Schnapps!

Jasper No you can't.

Evan has no idea what's going on.

Evan Um. Sorry. I thought that you guys were gonna . . .
I thought you guys were gonna drink.

KJ (*to Jasper*) Are you kidding?

Jasper doesn't respond.

JESUS.
I'm . . . this is unbelievable.
You're treating me like a child.

Jasper does not budge. KJ walks over to the recycling bin and kicks it.

FUCK!

Short pause.

This is so fucking pointless. I could just march over to the liquor store and buy whatever the fuck I want.
I'm thirty fucking years old!

Jasper Do it.
I'll just go home.

KJ You wouldn't fucking *know*!

Jasper Oh yes I would, my friend. Yes I would.

A pause.

Last time KJ started drinking he went off his meds and starting doing *this* to random people on the street.

He walks over to Evan.

KJ Don't do it, you asshole.

Jasper makes a little beak with his fingers and zaps Evan with it on his arm. Evan is startled.

Jasper *Zhoop. Zhoop. Zhoop. Zhoop.*

KJ . . . Fuck you.

Jasper goes back over to one of the plastic chairs and sits down. He takes out his cigarettes and lights one.

Jasper What else you got, Shelmerdine?

Evan Um . . .

Evan reaches into his backpack.

This is kind of dumb. But I thought I'd just . . .
I brought sparklers?

Evan takes out a box of sparklers.

I mean, they're old. They're from like two years ago.

Jasper SHPAHKLAHS!

Evan isn't sure how to respond to this.

I'm sorry. That sounded like I was imitating a Jewish
person or something.
'SHPAHKLAHS!'
. . . I have no problems with Jews, though.

Evan Um. Okay.

Jasper KJ might be like one-eighth Jewish or something,
right, KJ?

*KJ, standing near the recycling bin, shakes his head
sullenly.*

Or was that just a Sandy Jano theory?
Mm. (*To Evan.*) Sandy Jano is KJ's fantastic mother,
with whom he still lives. She's a little, ah, how shall we
say it, New-Agey? She's into the New Age? And she like
became obsessed with tracing their ancestry back and
proving they were Jewish or something.
It didn't really work, though, did it, KJ?

No response.

They're like Lutherans.

Pause.

I'm one-sixteenth Cherokee.

Evan No way.

Jasper . . . And KJ here has dreams that he's black.

Evan isn't sure whether he's supposed to find this funny or not. He looks at KJ, whose face is somewhat inscrutable.

Tell him.

KJ doesn't respond.

Tell him about the dream.

KJ continues to give no response.

Like two months ago KJ had this dream that he was like . . . that he was black. He comes to me and he tells me this. And I was like: wait. How'd you know in the dream that you were black? Did you like look in a mirror or something? And he was like: no. I was just hanging out with a bunch of black people and we were like all having a really good time together and laughing and I felt really, um, accepted –

KJ, despite himself, cracks a smile.

– and they all really liked me and then I realised that *I* was black. That I was one of them.

KJ And I was really happy.

Jasper . . . And he was really happy.

Pause. KJ and Jasper giggle.

Evan Um. That's kinda weird.

The sound of a distant, muffled explosion. The sky is significantly darker at this point.

(*Forgetting to be cool.*) Oh wow.

A pause.

I like forgot it was the Fourth of July for a second.

Another pause. Jasper looks at his watch.

Jasper They won't happen for at least another ten minutes.

No one knows what to say.

KJ Music!

Jasper Already?

KJ Frogmen.

KJ runs over to the corner and unbuckles the guitar case. He removes an acoustic guitar.

Jasper Lemme eat a brownie first.

Jasper grabs a brownie out of Evan's Tupperware, stuffs it in his mouth, and swallows it.

Okay.

KJ hands him the guitar and sits down next to him in a plastic chair.

(*To KJ.*) Do you want to give some kind of introduction? Explanation?

KJ shakes his head. Jasper nods and starts playing the opening chords to the song. He underscores the following monologue/dialogue with the opening chords. He speaks in that rhythmic way people speak over guitar chords. Weirdly, it opens him up a little.

(*To Evan.*) This is a very old song. Actually our oldest song.
Vintage Kevin Jano.
So.
When was this.
Shortly after we met.
KJ was a recent UVM dropout
and I never graduated from high school.

Evan Did you go to SHS, too?

Jasper Fuck no. I grew up in Alstead. You know where that is?

Evan shakes his head.

Jasper New Hampshire. It's a shithole.
There's nothing. There's a fucking war memorial and a soda fountain and that's it. Trailer trash.
I am a living piece of trailer trash.
Anyway
Moving on
KJ's a college dropout, I'm a street urchin, and:
we meet.
In Vermont.
In this town.
And two weeks later
KJ writes this song
and comes to me
and says:
you make up the music
you make up the chords.
(*After a pause, to KJ.*) You want to sing this alone?

KJ Frogmen sing together.

Jasper nods, plays the opening chords a few more times, and then they sing. During the song the sun sets completely, and by the end they are in the dark, lit only by the moon and perhaps a dim outdoor light on the patio.

Jasper *and* **KJ**
From Sagamore to Ogden
Come the slimy frogmen
They jiggle and jangle through the angle
From the bridge to the ridge and under the fridge
The frogmen come with bottles of rum.

KJ
(Mmm rum)

Jasper *and* **KJ**
Macho comacho threw the first shindig
Where the fat lady ate all the ring dings
The young ones ate like rabbits
And dreamt of Lake Placid
(The frogmen ate frog sticks frog cake and frog acid)
From under a landing came Butch and his bandmates
They played multiple sets of
Benny and the Jets
And we all placed bets
Yeah
With purple cigarettes
and the party was fine till quarter past nine
From up in Maine to down in Spain
The frogmen crew blew their brains
From frick to frack
I flick my ash
From dust to dust
I eat your crust
Frogmen, frogmen
No matter where they go
they leave time for the wildlife
Frogmen, frogmen
They march to and fro to the drum and fife
Yeah
From Sagamore to Ogden.

*The fireworks begin. The noise is powerful, despite the
fact that it's coming from a distance. KJ and Jasper
stop singing. They all sit and listen, in silence. The
explosions build over the next minute or so the way
that fireworks do, rising to some sort of climax, then
fizzling out, then rising again, then working up to a
series of short and manic bursts.*

At some point, probably about twenty seconds in, KJ gets up and starts dancing. He dances in weird little circles around the patio.
Jasper and Evan watch him. The fireworks continue.

Jasper You got any friends at SHS, Shelmerdine?

Evan shakes his head peacefully.

Evan No.

They watch KJ dance to the fireworks. After a while:

KJ (*still dancing*)
I NEED A SPARKLER!

Evan gets a sparkler out of the box. Jasper lights it and hands it to KJ. They flinch and move back as it rains down light.
KJ dances with the sparkler.
They watch him.
After a little while, quietly:

Jasper Don't forget to come back from band camp, Shelmerdine.

Evan Um. It's not technically band camp.

The fireworks reach their climax.

KJ (*referring to the sparkler*) It's going out it's going out it's going out!

The sparkler goes out.
Darkness.
End of Act One.

Act Two

The same set. KJ is sitting by himself, with a cup of tea.
He sits by himself, thinking.
He sits by himself for a long time.
This should be at least twenty seconds.
Finally he says:

KJ If P then Q.

Then more silence. More sitting by himself. Then Evan
enters from the side with his backpack, radiant.

Evan Hey!

KJ . . . Hey!

Pause.

Welcome back from band camp!

Evan Thanks.
Yeah.

Another pause that goes on a little too long.

KJ Did you have a good time?

Evan Yeah. Actually.
It was pretty cool. I, like, I don't know. It was cool.
The kids were cute or whatever. And I, like – yeah. The
other C-I-Ts were cool.

Pause.

I met a girl, actually.

KJ Excellent.

Evan Yeah. I mean, whatever. It was just like a week. But she was pretty cool.

Pause.

Nicole.

KJ Nic*ole.*

Evan Yeah. She's like a violist.
I don't know.
She lives in Boston.
So if I wanted to visit her I'd have to like drive three hours. So I don't know.
It was cool, though.

Pause.

I mean, it's kind of humiliating that it's taken me this long, but . . .
It's kind of humiliating.

KJ No. That's beautiful, man.

Pause.

Did you finger her pussy?

Evan blanches a little.

Oh. Sorry. Is that inappropriate?

Evan No. Um. I mean. Yeah. I did.
Yeah.

KJ . . . Great!

Evan Seventeen is like kind of pathetic, though, right? I mean, that it's happening for the first time, like, now?

KJ There are no rules, man.

Evan Yeah.
I mean.
When was your first . . . whatever? Kiss. / Or –

KJ Ah . . . let's see. My first kiss I was, like, fourteen?

Evan nods.

It was with this like sixteen-year-old chick at an Allman Brothers show. And I was totally tweaked out just to like kiss her but then she tried to give me a blow job in a Porto Potty and my like little hairless dick like didn't respond and I was totally humiliated.

Evan Oh man.

KJ And then I dated this like younger girl when I was in high school, she was like a freshman and I was a senior and I think I kind of fucked with her head. We had sex and like now looking back I'm not sure that she was like totally ready, you know? Then I fuckin' cheated on her with this girl at a Chess Championship and we like had mindblowing sex or whatever, me and the chess girl, and then I made the mistake of like coming back home and like *telling* her or whatever to like get it off my chest and right after I told her she like crumpled in this little like . . .

He makes a vague gesture and waits for the word to come.

. . . *heap* on the ground and she like cried and cried but she stayed with me and then I broke up with her anyway right before I went off to UVM.

So yeah.

Evan Wow.

KJ Bleak, man. It was bleak.

Evan When did you have your like first serious girlfriend?

KJ Ah . . .

KJ shrugs uncomfortably.

Evan At UVM?

KJ Well. Sophomore year I fucked this girl in my interdisciplinary seminar but then I dropped out at the beginning of junior year.

A weird pause.

Yeah. I'm not really interested in, like . . . I don't know. Serious shit or whatever.

Another weird pause.

Evan Um. Cool. Well. I should probably go inside. I'm workin' the three-to-ten.

KJ Awesome.

Evan Maybe I'll see you guys tomorrow.

KJ Wanna hear a song?

Evan looks at his watch.

Evan Um. Sure. Yeah. I should go inside in like, a / minute, but –

KJ starts singing.

KJ
Drawing on the strength of the community
A period of spiritual activity
Ango
A Japanese word
That literally means
A peaceful dwelling
Increasing in vigour and clarity
Unfolding new sections of our neighbourhood
Among a small band of students
Collective commitment
To realisation
Relaxation
Translating into stimulation

Practising zazen in our zendo
Upon an altar in my dojo
I am a sensei
I am a sensei.

Evan (*edging towards the door*) That's awesome.

KJ It's not over.

In our city of harmony
This incredible nation
Circled over the world around us
Returns home with us
The first time I asked the incense
Sustain the ongoing delusion
Social status quo
Intuitive energy flow
I am a sensei.

A pause.

Evan Cool.

KJ Thanks.

Evan Are you, like, a Buddhist?

KJ You could say that.
You could say that.

Pause.

Evan Um. See ya later, KJ.

Evan exits into the coffee shop.
   KJ sits by himself. He thinks hard about something, and then, upon realising something else, smiles. Then he goes back to thinking again.
   Blackout.

SCENE TWO

KJ is standing next to the back door, leaning up against the wall. He is humming quietly to himself. It looks a little like he's waiting to surprise someone.

After a while, Evan comes out through the back door in his white apron, lugging a full garbage bag. He starts when he sees KJ.

Evan Oh. Wow!

KJ giggles.

You scared me. Kind of.

They stand there for a second, and then Evan walks over to the garbage bin, opens it, and throws the garbage bag in. Then he tries leaning casually against the garbage bin, but it's too uncomfortable. He stands up straight, stuffs his hands in his pockets, and stands there while KJ gazes at him, smiling.

I have a five-minute break.

KJ claps his hands.

KJ Yay!!!

Evan Where's Jasper?

KJ He's sick.

Evan Oh man. That sucks.

KJ Yeah.

Evan Does he have like a cold? Or / like –

KJ Yup.

A long pause. They are both at a loss. Evan decides to try sitting in one of the plastic chairs. He does so.

KJ stays by the door. Silence for a while.

(*With exaggerated excitement.*) So are you gonna go to college?!

Evan Um. Yeah. Next year? Yeah. I think so.

KJ Where?

Evan Um. I don't know. I mean, wherever I get in I guess? I don't know. I'm kind of interested in Bates?

KJ Never heard of it.

Evan Yeah. It's kind of small. It's in Maine.

Pause.

You dropped out, right?

KJ nods.

Why? Um. If it's not rude to ask.

KJ I had a breakdown. I don't know. I wouldn't really call it a breakdown.

A pause.

Evan Okay. Cool.

KJ College is bullshit, though.
    If you're like . . . I mean, if you've like . . . if you're the real thing, or if you've got like . . . college is just like pointless.

Evan nods.

Jasper didn't go to college.

Evan Yeah.

Pause.

Did you have like a major?

KJ Double Major. Math and Philosophy.

Evan Oh cool! Philosophy is cool. I mean, I don't know anything about it.

KJ Ever heard of propositional calculus?

Evan No. I mean. I haven't – I'm taking pre-calc next year.

KJ Propositional calculus is different from regular calculus, my little friend. It's Logic.

Evan nods, confused.

I was gonna write my thesis on it.
    You woulda loved it.

Evan What was it . . . what is it, / like –

KJ You know about truth tables?

Evan shakes his head.

No? Okay. Well.

KJ scratches his beard thoughtfully.

It's like: If P then Q, then, you know, Truth.
    Or it's like: If P then *not* Q.
    Or it's like: P and Q. Or P *or* Q.
    But when it gets interesting is when you try figure out what can be a P and Q in the first place.

A pause.

So okay. Let's say P is: 'I'm a wizard.' And Q is: 'The wizard is yellow.' Then, uh . . .
    You have to figure out if there's even such thing as a . . .

KJ trying to think. A long pause. Evan is starting to feel uncomfortable.

Evan Um –

KJ Or:
Let's say you're feeling sad, right? You're feeling sad.

Evan Okay.

KJ And you like look at your own sadness. From like above. And that's how you're able to say, you know: 'I feel sad.'

Evan Okay.

KJ But like: what do you – which of your senses, like – how do you *do* that?

Pause.

Or like: or: or:
J, right? Picture the letter J. As in Jasper.

Evan . . . Okay.

KJ And then picture another J. Sitting next to it.

Evan nods.

And I say to you: 'J is the same thing as J.'

Evan Okay.

KJ But *how do you prove that?*

A pause.

Evan Um.

Short pause.

Because they look like each other?

KJ EXACTLY!
That was my point.
That was the gist of my thesis.

Pause.

Evan Um. I should probably go back inside.

Evan starts to head back inside.

KJ I love you, Shelmerdine.

Evan stops in his tracks, terrified. Is he supposed to say it back? A long pause while KJ gazes at him. Finally:

Evan Um. I love you too.

KJ Just kidding.

Another pause.

Just kidding!

Evan Yeah. Um. Me too.

Evan hesitates, then goes back inside the coffee shop. KJ doesn't move.
 Blackout.

SCENE THREE

The same day. Evening.
 KJ has not left. He is lying across two chairs, sleeping. There are a couple of tiny liquor bottles at his feet.
 Evan comes out with his backpack on. He is closing up the café.

Evan Oh shit.

Evan stands there looking at KJ for while. He approaches him and tries poking him very lightly. Nothing happens. He tries poking him harder. After a few seconds, KJ opens his eyes but does not move.

KJ Was I snoring?

Evan No.

A pause.

Evan Is. Um. Is everything okay?

KJ Do you like Jasper more than me?

Evan Um.
No.
No!

KJ Every time I see you you want to know if Jasper's here.

Evan That's because Jasper is usually / here.

KJ He's sick!

Evan I know. I'm sorry.

Pause.

KJ I wanna kill myself.

Evan Oh shit.

Evan sits down near KJ on a plastic chair, takes out his cell phone and dials.

Mom.
I'm gonna be late for dinner.

Short pause.

Um . . . this guy I work with is upset.

Short pause.

He broke up with his girlfriend.

Pause.

Please don't ask me that. Please don't ask me that. Please don't ask me that.

Short pause.

Please don't ask me that.
I don't care.
I don't care.
Okay.

Evan hangs up. KJ is still lying across the chairs.

I hate her.

KJ Whoa.

Evan She like – she does this thing? She does this thing where she like asks what kind of – like if I want cauliflower or carrots with dinner and then if I like tell her carrots she's like, well, your father doesn't – and it's just like whatever I say she like contradicts me and I'm just like –
Never mind. It's stupid.

KJ nods understandingly.

KJ Yeah.
This one time . . .
This one time I couldn't stop saying this one word? I was like obsessed with this word. I would just walk around whispering it to myself.
I was a little kid. I was like five.
I would walk around all day saying:
(*He whispers softly.*) Ladder. Ladder. Ladder.

Evan Ladder? Like what you climb on?

KJ nods.

KJ I couldn't stop saying it. I started like whispering it to myself at night and I wouldn't be able to fall asleep. And finally one night my mom got into my bed with me and she was like: you can say it for as long and as loud as you want and I'll hold your hand the whole time.
And I was like: okay.
And I just went:
Ladder.
Ladder.
Ladder.
Ladder.

Ladder.
Ladder.
Ladder. Ladder. Ladder. Ladder. Ladder. Ladder.
Ladder. Ladder. Ladder. Ladder. Ladder. Ladder. Ladder.
Ladder. Ladder. Ladder. Ladder. Ladder. Ladder. Ladder.
Ladder. Ladder. Ladder. Ladder. Ladder. Ladder. Ladder.
Ladder. Ladder. Ladder. Ladder. Ladder. Ladder. Ladder.
Ladder. Ladder. Ladder. Ladder. Ladder. Ladder. Ladder.
Ladder. Ladder. Ladder. Ladder. Ladder. Ladder. Ladder.
Ladder. Ladder. Ladder. Ladder. Ladder. Ladder. Ladder.
Ladder. Ladder. Ladder. Ladder. Ladder. Ladder. Ladder.
Ladder. Ladder. Ladder. Ladder. Ladder. Ladder. Ladder.
Ladder. Ladder. Ladder. Ladder. Ladder. Ladder. Ladder.
Ladder. Ladder. Ladder. Ladder. Ladder. Ladder. Ladder.
Ladder. Ladder. Ladder. Ladder. Ladder. Ladder. Ladder.
Ladder. Ladder. Ladder.

He has begun to cry by this point.

Ladder. Ladder. Ladder. Ladder. Ladder. Ladder. Ladder.
Ladder. Ladder. Ladder. Ladder. Ladder. Ladder. Ladder.
Ladder. Ladder. Ladder. Ladder. Ladder. Ladder.
Ladder. Ladder. Ladder. Ladder. Ladder. Ladder.
Ladder. Ladder. Ladder. Ladder. Ladder. Ladder. Ladder.
Ladder.

Pause.

. . . And then I stopped.

Pause. Evan is frozen in place.

Evan Um.

A long pause.

KJ He died.

Evan looks at him uncomprehendingly. Pause.

Jasper died.

Pause.

Evan . . . No he didn't.

KJ He died a week ago.

Pause.

Evan No.

KJ nods.

Come on. Stop it.

A pause.

No, he didn't.

Silence.

Why are you . . . stop fucking with me.

Pause.

You just said he was sick!

KJ I'm sorry.
I'm really really sorry.

Evan Why are you saying that?!

KJ shrugs. Silence.

KJ Isn't that weird?
That he died?
I just think it's so weird.

Evan walks over to the big recycling bin and tries to knock it over. But this is hard to do. The recycling bin is very, very heavy. It takes Evan a long time. For a while, it seems like he's not going to be able to do it. Then, finally, he tips it over. The sound of glass bottles falling. Maybe a few roll out onto the ground.
    Evan walks inside.
    KJ is alone.
    After a long time Evan walks out again. He is holding an oatmeal raisin cookie.

Evan What did he die of?

KJ He died.

Evan *What* did he die of?!

Pause.

Are you fucking with me? You can't . . . you have to tell me if you're fucking with me!

KJ He died in his sleep. I think. He died in his room. He was shooting up. He died.

Evan He was *what?*

KJ He wasn't like . . . he'd only done it a couple of times before. He was just . . . it was an accident.

Evan Were you *there?*

KJ shakes his head.

That doesn't make any sense!

Pause.

KJ It's okay if you can't cry.

Evan begins to cry.

Evan Oh my God.
I have to go home.
I have to go home.

KJ Okay.

Evan I have to go home. I'm sorry. I don't know why I have this cookie.
I have to go home.

*Evan puts his cookie down on the table and leaves.
KJ is alone.
Eventually he starts singing, softly and slowly.*

KJ

Zane
Sits
By a brook
A little stream
In a nook
In a cranny with his krammy
He sits by a brook
And he looooks
In the water
That falls down the rocks –

KJ notices the fallen recycling bin. He stops singing and walks over to it. He tries to right it. It takes a very long time, but he succeeds. He stares at it for a while, then lays his hand on top of it.
   Blackout.

SCENE FOUR

The next day.
   Evan is standing outside by himself, on a break. He wears his white apron. He looks around furtively, and then he takes a pack of cigarettes out of his pocket. He tries tapping the pack of cigarettes against his palm, a little unsure of what direction to tap it in. Then he unwraps it, with some difficulty. Then he takes out a cigarette. Then he takes out a book of matches from his pocket. He lights the cigarette.
   This is the first time in his life he has ever bought a pack of cigarettes and this is the first time in his life that he has ever smoked a cigarette by himself.
   There is a certain bittersweet joy in it.
   While he smokes, he gazes around, looking for KJ.
   After a little while, Evan takes out his cell phone and he dials. He waits, then:

Evan Hey.
It's Evan.
How are you?
Um.
I'm smoking a cigarette.

Pause.

I'm calling because I want to know how your recital thing
went and if they gave you the first part for Pachelbel's or
if you had to play the other part.
I bet you were good. Either way.
Um.

Pause.

I'm also calling because my friend died? Um. I know that
sounds really dramatic but um. My friend died. I don't
know. Um. He was like a genius and like a novelist and
he died of a drug overdose.
He was like one of my best friends.
I'm um . . .
I'd like to come visit you in Boston.
He's the only person I um . . .
My grandparents died when I was a baby.
Okay. Sorry this message is rambly.

Evan hangs up.
He stubs out his cigarette.
He waits for KJ, in vain.
A minute passes.
Blackout.

SCENE FIVE

The set is empty.
After a few seconds KJ enters, with Jasper's guitar case
on his back.

It's a bit startling to see him enter because we have only seen him attached to the picnic table and plastic chairs up until this point.

KJ puts his guitar case down and sits in one of the plastic chairs. He is wearing shorts and sneakers and sunglasses. He sits there for a while, in the sunlight, and then he bends down and unlaces his shoe. He turns his shoe upside down.

A pebble falls out onto the ground and makes a small noise.

KJ doesn't put his shoe back on.

He takes a paperback book out of his bag. He flips through it and opens to a page and starts reading it.

Evan appears at the back door, peeks out, and sees KJ. He opens the door and walks out. He is wearing his white apron. KJ keeps reading. Evan doesn't know what to do. He takes out his pack of cigarettes and lights one. He is much better at smoking by this point. Evan smokes while KJ reads.

Eventually:

Evan Hey.

KJ Hey.

Evan I haven't seen you for a few days.

KJ Yeah.

Pause.

I might be moving.

Evan Oh. Wow. Um. Really?

KJ I might be. I'm thinking about it.

Evan Where?

KJ I have a list of places.
I'm trying to decide.

Short pause.

Wanna hear?

Evan Yeah.

KJ wrenches a small, wrinkled, soggy piece of paper out of his pocket.

KJ These are just some ideas.
Okay. (*He reads.*) Austin, Texas.

Evan Oh cool. It's supposed to be cool down there.

KJ It's high on the list.
Iowa City.
Olympia, Washington.
Taos. I don't know if I said that right.
Amherst, Massachusetts.
Orion's wind farm.
Seattle.

Evan What's Orion's wind farm?

KJ Oh. Uh. This guy? Jasper's old weed dealer? He lives on like a wind farm in Marshfield.

Evan What's a wind farm?

KJ It's like . . . it's like the white windmill things by the side of the road. The big uh . . . like the / spinny –

Evan Oh yeah.

KJ (*going back to the paper*) Eureka, California.

Evan How does he *live* there?

KJ (*ignoring him*) Eureka, California.
Asheville. Question mark.
Commune in Virginia where they make hammocks, find out name.
     . . . Can't read my own handwriting. Resnick? Redding?
This one's a stretch: Winnipeg?

Evan Where's that?

KJ It's in the Canadian province of Manitoba? I believe.

Pause.

That's it.

Evan Those all sound cool.

KJ Yeah.
I'm thinkin' about it. I don't know. Sandy Jano is
against the idea. But.

Evan stubs out his cigarette on the ground.

. . . Smoker.

Evan Yeah. I guess. I mean, hopefully. Not.

Pause.

Um. I'm sorry I, um. Ran away. Or whatever. On
Wednesday.

KJ nods.

Evan Is there gonna be a funeral? 'Cause I'd really / like –

KJ It was last week.

Evan nods. A long pause.

Evan He was so, um, cool.

A self-conscious pause.

I kind of feel like a completely different . . .

*Evan shakes his head tearily and can't finish his
sentence.*
KJ looks at him for a little while.

KJ Come here.

Evan walks over to him.

Kneel down.

Evan tentatively knees down.

I'm going to bless you. I'm going to remove your toxins.

KJ puts his fingers together and touches Evan's cheek.
(*Quietly.*) Zhoop.

Pause.

That's it.
You can stand up again.

Evan stands up again.

Evan Um. KJ? I should / tell you –

KJ I'm sending his novel out. It was almost finished so I thought they could publish it as, like. You know. An unfinished thing.

Evan Oh. Cool.

KJ Yeah. I'm just like looking in the like, book jackets of all my mom's books and I'm like: all right. Farrar Stroose and Geeroosh. Union Square. I'll send it to you.

Evan Don't you like need an agent or something?

KJ shrugs and lifts up the book in his lap. It is Bukowski's The Last Night of the Earth.

KJ Did *Bukowski* have an agent?

Evan Yeah. I don't know.

Short pause.

I'm reading some of his . . . I took out, um . . . I'm reading *Ham on Rye*? And um – yeah. *Love Is a Dog from Hell.*

KJ You like it?

Evan Yeah. Yeah. He like. It's, um. It's great. He says 'cunt' a lot.

63

KJ Yeah!

Evan . . . Yeah.

Pause.

Um.

  KJ?

KJ Yes.

Evan Rahna came back yesterday.
  I guess she was on vacation?

KJ Uh huh.

Evan And she said you guys, um . . . she said that you
can't be back here. And she was really, um, mad. And I
explained to her about, um . . . about what, um,
happened while I was gone –

  KJ slowly starts putting his shoe back on.

– but she was really pissed at me and she told the
manager which was really stupid of her but she told him
and he said that, um, that you guys, that, um, you, can't
be here any more. I mean, nobody's supposed to be back
here except for staff.

  KJ nods.

. . . And I got really mad and I like argued with him and
I was like: he's not *doing* anything, but um they found
um those liquor bottles I guess and apparently Jasper
once um *peed* out here or something so they um . . .

  He fades out. KJ nods.

He's coming back tomorrow and he's gonna be check / ing
all the –

KJ It's cool.

64

Evan You can start coming inside if you want.
I can make you free tea.

KJ Yeah. I don't know. They always play that Ani DiFranco shit inside.

Evan . . . Yeah.

KJ Uh.

Evan You can stay as late as you want today! I mean. Nobody's gonna check.

Pause.

I should go probably go back inside in a minute.

KJ Yeah.

A pause.

I have a present for you.

KJ points to the guitar case.

I don't know how to play, so.
It's his guitar.

Evan I can't take that.

KJ It's for you. His roommates didn't want it.

Evan . . . I don't know.

KJ Do you already have one?

Evan Um. No. I mean, my mom has a really crappy one and I play that sometimes.

KJ Take it. It's pretty good. He stole it from some yuppie asshole in Burlington.

Evan looks at it. He bends down and unbuckles the case. He takes out the guitar. He looks at it. He holds it.

Try it.

Evan I'm not very good.

Evan plays a few halting chords.

KJ Yeah!!
Yes.

Evan smiles a little.

Evan I feel weird taking it.

Pause.

Okay. I mean. Thank you.

KJ Thank Joseph Yoseph. Thank the Limp Handshakes.

Evan Okay.

KJ Thank The Aliens.

Evan Okay.

KJ Play something!

Evan I should go back inside.

KJ Play something first!

Evan Um.

Evan thinks.

KJ Don't think!

Evan Um.

Evan hesitates, and then messily starts playing the first few chords of 'If I Had a Hammer'.

(*Singing softly.*)
If I had a hammer, I'd hammer / in –

KJ No covers!

Evan stops playing.

Evan Oh. Um. Sorry.

I don't know any, um . . . I don't have any, like, originals. I don't write music.

KJ Why not?

Evan Um. I don't know. I don't think I'm good enough. I don't know. I'm not like a genius musically or anything.

KJ How do you know?

Evan shrugs.

I'm a genius. *Jasper* was a genius.

Evan . . . Yeah.

KJ Maybe you're a genius too!

Pause.

Evan Yeah.

Pause.

Um. I should probably go back inside.

KJ Play 'The Hammer Song'.

Pause.

KJ Play 'The Hammer Song'!

Evan Really?

KJ Play it.

Evan looks anxiously towards the back door, and then starts playing 'If I Had a Hammer'. The first verse is painful – Evan's voice is thin and slightly out-of-tune, and he strums haltingly and botches a few of the chords. Then he takes in a long, shaky breath and starts playing the second verse. He gets a little better. His voice grows stronger and clearer. By the time he

*hits the third verse ('If I had a song'), Evan is kind of
playing the shit out of 'If I Had A Hammer.' The third
verse ends.*
   A pause.
   Evan puts down the guitar, crimson-faced.

Evan
   Um. Yeah.
   It's kind of a stupid song. I don't even know what it
means.

KJ . . . That was awesome.

Evan I kind of fucked it up.

KJ You're gonna go far, man.

Evan Come on.

KJ I'm not kidding.
   You're gonna go far.

Evan . . . Yeah?

KJ Yeah.

   Evan tries not to smile. But then he does.
      They stand there.
      Blackout.
      End of play.